*To my three sons: Les, Philip, and David,
in whom the past and future meet.*

Circling Home

# Scripta humanistica

Directed by
BRUNO M. DAMIANI
The Catholic University of America

# Circling Home

Cheryl Romney-Brown

Scripta humanistica

53

Romney-Brown, Cheryl.
    Circling Home / Cheryl Romney-Brown.
        p. cm. — (Scripta Humanistica ; 53)
    ISBN 0-916379-59-0 : $22.50
    I. Title. II. Series: Scripta Humanistica (Series) ; 53.
PS3568.05654C5   1989      89-6127
811'.54—dc20      CIP


                    *Publisher and Distributor:*
                    **SCRIPTA HUMANISTICA**
                        1383 Kersey Lane
                Potomac, Maryland 20854 U.S.A.


                    © Cheryl Romney-Brown
        Library of Congress Catalog Card Number 89-6127
        International Standard Book Number 0-916379-59-0

Pamela Soldwedel's sculpture "Search"

*"We shall not cease from exploration.*
*And the end of all our exploring*
*will be to arrive where we started.*
*And know the place for the first time."*

*"LITTLE GIDDING"*    *T. S. Eliot*

# Table of Contents

## II. SHATTERED HOUSES

## III. CIRCLING HOME

# Foreword
## Senator Eugene McCarthy

Poets are at work in the United States despite all the materialism, crassness, continuous demands for instant judgment, over-simplification, superficiality — all of the marks which social critics and historians lay upon our culture.

The poets are looking inward and outward, forward and backward; Sometimes, simply being and thinking in the "now."

There are for all poets two dangerous Points of Passage, the first in which the poet seeks the poem in the "terra terribilia" in which, according to the ancient map makers:

All is nothing
but dry and desert sands
inhabited only by wild creatures
or dark impassable bogs
of Scythian cold
or frozen sea
beyond which there is nothing
but monstrous and tragical fiction.
There the poets
and inventors of fables dwell.

1

The second is at the Point of Publication. Most poets, even those who are well established, ordained as it were by having been called poets by other poets, and cleared by critics, are hesitant, apprehensive, even fearful over the publication not only of a volume of new poems, but of a single new poem. The risk and fear, as noted by Ferlinghetti, is comparable to that of the acrobat and the high wire performer. The poet reveals or publishes what he or she has found, exposing self and poem to ridicule, scorn, rejection, and worst of all, indifference.

In this volume of poems, Cheryl Romney-Brown has ventured into the terra terribilia of self and past, has searched, and sifted, and refined experience, sought out threatening and dangerous themes, especially those to be found in the Mormon church into which she was born, carrying names notable in Mormon history — Romney and Brown, companion names to those of Joseph Smith and Brigham Young — men driven or drawn by a revelation, an American one, given to men who in the faith that flowed from that revelation, moved ever westward to Utah, and even on to Mexico in search of a place where they could live their beliefs.

The most compelling of poems in this book are about the women who accompanied, followed, and sustained the prophets; of love and the testing of it; of faith, in arranged and in polygamous marriages; and of subtle undercurrents of memory or of imagining of a different past, and of a different future, a circling.

In this volume Cheryl Romney-Brown returns from the terra terribilia and courageously joins the company of poets in publishing what she has seen, and done, and thought, willing to be judged, as Yeats said, thinned out "like milk spilt on a stone."

Eugene J. McCarthy

March 1, 1989

# Preface

I did not seek to write poetry; much to my great joy, it found me. Several years ago, while I was visiting London, an extraordinary thing happened: one night I was unable to go to sleep because a rhyme kept spinning in my head, much as a familiar tune takes possession and haunts until it wears itself out. But in this case, the tune was my own. As the night wore on, I realized that there would be no sleep until I quieted this beguiling muse. Therefore, I sat down and began to write. Much to my amazement, a verse emerged. Almost immediately my head was bursting with another. I wrote that one down too. And so they continued for the duration of my trip at the rate of four or five a day. It was almost as if someone released a geyser of words, but the exciting thing was that each was fully formed with a beginning, middle, and an end — a totality — a poem, albeit one that needed work.

Since then, the muse's visits have slowed down; I have worked hard to learn and refine my craft, also to enrich my poetic vocabulary. I am very fortunate to have the support and wisdom of gifted writers who have since become good friends.

My grateful thanks goes to Evelyn Nef and Gladys Chilton, who first recognized my potential as a poet and gave me the confidence to begin. Also, I was very fortunate to be working on a master's degree in a superb academic setting at the time, Georgetown University. I want to thank: Paul Betz,

Roland Flint, Shirley Cochrane, Phyllis O'Callahan, and Jean Eswein, whose belief and encouragement spurred me on. I am greatly appreciative of Elizabeth Sullam, Carolyn Kreiter-Kurylo, Gabriele Glang, Betty Parry, Sharon Costello, Charles Sullivan, Stacy Tuthill, William Claire, and Rick Peabody, whose love and knowledge of poetry has greatly nourished me; also, their generous sharing has been invaluable. I want to thank splendid friends whose support I am deeply grateful for: Jaan Whitehead, E. William Henry, Alice Tarnowski, Cathy Herter, John Culman, Diana Cashen, Patricia Di Gorgio, Maryann Opperman, Elizabeth Griffinger, Kathy Kenety, Gail and Jack Anderson, Dielle Fleischman, Richard Hueber, and Elizabeth Worrall among others who are too numerous to mention. And to my dear friends, Ann and Dick Otter, who so graciously gave me the use of their lovely home in Sonoma, California, to finish this manuscript, I extend a very special thank you. And finally, I am passionately indebted to my family: my sister, Linda Woodhouse; Romney and Brown relatives, who so generously responded with stories of our ancestors; and my three sons, Leslie, Philip, and David, who are my loving mainstays.

*Cheryl Romney-Brown*

# I.  PIONEERS

*"Our ancestors toiled, suffered and died that their
children might inherit the promise"*

Edward Ridpath

## An Heirloom from Utah Pioneer Days

Hidden away in a drawer
beneath my lace nightgown
lies Great Grandmother's
rose sachet.

An extravagant luxury
born in the heart
of the desert. Cuttings
cradled across endless
plains, petals dried
from prized bushes,
lovingly nurtured
from parched sand.

Rare rose petals to saturate
a bridal bower. Musky
scent to soften hungry
children's screams.
Opiate to salve
broken promises,
unfulfilled dreams.
Like frankincense
and myrrh, a celebration
of hope

6

in the desert
passed from mother
to daughter, mother
to daughter, mother
to daughter.

At night, in my lace
gown, I remember
my future.

## Photographs

### 1 (1846)

In the rain-soaked crowd
at the end of the wharf,
she clutches the loden cape
around her frail body.
It whips in the sea wind.
She presses a handkerchief
to wet cheeks.
Her determined hand
once again brushes
the dark hair away
from stinging lids.
These eyes must seize
his silhouette,
burn forever the curve
of her first-born's
cleft chin into her mind.
As the tall ship escapes
the English dock, she lets
go of the cape, waves.
Her palm at first beats
the air like hummingbird's
wings, but then slows down

like the pendulum on death's
clock. The small hand slaps
at the wind long after
the ship has sailed beyond sight,
toward Zion, God, America.
Dusk slips into the ship's empty
berth. The crowd deserts
the angry sea. Her worn body alone
faces west.

The heaving deck shudders
with shivering passengers
reluctant to go below
as they capture their last look
at family, wave their farewell
to England. George Romney stands erect
at the stern, a man about twenty,
garbed in black, clutching "the Book
of Mormon" in both hands. His tearless
face, open with faith, stares west.

## 2 (1989)

My now grown-up son's picture captures
his blond curls, blue eyes. A broad
smile floods his two-year-old face.
Snapped before he rocked with pain:
ear infections, allergies, dyslexia.

Last year frozen water pipes burst, deluging
the basement. All of our family albums
ruined. I rummage in my large black
purse trying to find the picture. My fingers
grasp only small change, paper clips,
a bright red lipstick, an old ball-point
pen.

## Inherit the Promise

1

Heaving wagons shadow the sun west
like toys pulled with golden cords
by an unknown giant, bend tall
grasses as the prow of a ship
parts the Atlantic. Only groans
from plodding oxen, the swish
of grass momentarily yielding
to man hang in the air. No queen bee
buzzes or swallow sings. Late afternoon
glows a bewitched pale yellow, transparent
green, then a violent red streak flashes
into sunset, muting to shades of raspberries
she picked in the Lake Windemere countryside.
A damp spot of the same hue ripens
on her pink gingham dress; new roundness
strains her bodice. The sunset glares.
Suddenly the sun abandons the sky.
Her eyes absorb the prairie: lifeless
under hulking shadows. No place to hide
as in the lush vales of England. Stars
begin sparking; one blazes across
the vaulting sky, then is swallowed
by blackness. She turns her head around,
gazes toward England.

2

Scraping of wagon wheels against
granite Rockies chills patience.
The wagon ahead lurches over
a boulder, then balks at the summit.
Settlers scramble to the edge
of Promontory Point to witness
a declaration. Joseph Smith throws
open his arms, pronounces in a booming
voice: "This is the place." Blood storms out
of her head. Brother Brown's arms
sweep her up. Before them lies
her hearthstone: a vast bone
wasteland ranges beyond sight, broken
only by a salt-burdened lake.

3

Her hand clutches tiny plants to her breast
as they crumble to dust. Her other hand yanks
locust out of her hair, the slick armor
almost impossible to grasp. Their whir sounds
like scolding voices from the scalding sun. Plagues
of locust strip fields of green. The children clutch

at their mother's petticoats, moan with hunger.
Her husband, smitten with duty, gallops headlong
to the Temple, to be sealed to another wife. These arid
days her mind dwells in the emerald shade
of the old oak in Windemere. She hears robins chirp,
smells purple hyacinths in bloom. Then clouds
appear on the skyline, roll rapidly toward her.
Was she to be embraced by a gathering of angels,
taken home so soon? White flapping wings encircle her.
Beyond horizons thousands of white birds sail in
blotting out scorch-light of midday sun. Seagulls
descend, gorge on locust. Days later bloated birds
flap back to the Pacific. The western rim of the earth
floods red-purple. She does not glance back;
only the Rockies are stone.

## For Pioneers

*Including my ancestor, Captain James Brown,*
*a Mormon pioneer, who founded Ogden, Utah.*

Perhaps,
when the white dust had settled
and the crimson sun of dusk
no longer seared the Great Salt Lake,
when the last blue ribbon of light
had wrapped the day's history,
been pulled tight over the earth's
edge toward Mexico, you took off
your soldier's medals, buried
your head in your young wife's
breasts and wept.

At last, settled in your retreat,
you had infinite time to identify,
count bleached skeletons hidden
in your mind: two wives, several
children, the Donner party, young
soldiers in your command, babies
and mothers starved in treks
across plains, believers
who could not survive winter Rockies.

14

In the rough comfort of the first log
cabin in the great basin, you looked beyond
your greening meadow, saw the parched
West stretched out like an albino
pony's skin. Endless miles of scorched
land, vacant skies waiting
for innocents to colonize.

## Mexican Pilgrimage

*The United States Militia surrounded the Great Salt Lake Basin
to imprison polygamous Latter Day Saints. Orson Pratt Brown
received a call to lead them to safety within a Mexican Mormon
colony. He married his first wife, Martha Romney, while there.
During their stay, the Mexican Revolution exploded into
flames in 1912.*

1

Grandmother,
muffled
in choke-necked linen waists,
consumed by voluminous
skirts, shielded children
beneath ample folds
of her imagination.
First of six polygamous
wives, she consented
to her husband
taking another
when the bishop
whispered all her babes
would die unless she
opened her heart
to a sister wife.

Her husband cast
her from her own
feather bed
the day his new young wife
floated over the threshold.
That night her tears baptized
clay floors where she lay,
dyeing them brimstone gray.

Racing wagon wheels struck
her first child's head.
She clasped the remains
of the skull over the brain,
rocking for endless
time. His tiny wasting
body was pried
from her locked
arms to shroud him
in her bridal linen
three days after he died.
The child's father,
seven days late,
allotted no time
to rein in streaking horses to save his firstborn son.

2

My father's young memory:
one scorched dawn, he stretched
his matchstick legs another inch
to point a heavy rifle
blindly through a narrow slit.
Each child prayed for war,
longed for rebels to gallop
in front of his aim
so he, alone, would make the first kill,
be blooded by night.
Yesterday an uncle had been dredged
up from their well. Stuffed
down the narrow shaft, he drowned
at midnight, poisoning
still waters by daybreak.
Pancho Villa's threat — that their own father,
if caught, would hang hours past death —
tightened the fingers caressing
the triggers. Revolutionaries scanning
seven guns across adobe facades,
unaware each was manned by a son
under twelve, scattered
as if they'd heard thunder cannonading
across the desert.

Later, he dreamed
of circling buzzards,
his father's
lengthening shadow
on a darkening mesquite tree.

## A Family Story

Noise rustled trees.
As she burst out the door,
an arrow pinned a dishrag
to her hand, palm to thigh.
A second sped through her heart.
The mother fell; her body draped
in long skirts hid the child.
The baby curled into a shell,
cocooned beneath an apron's
billowing folds. Indians looted
the adobe casa, leaving a lone
scout outside. Looking for gold,
one ripped open a pillow; feathers
filled the air. Shrieking, they slit
open all bedding, prancing.
The brave deserted his watch,
joined the spree. Two brothers
stowed in furrows beneath coops
caught their sister's glazed
look. She cowered; her brothers
scooped her up, racing beyond
the hill's bend. The Indians followed.

While sharing stories at their wedding,
Mother gasped, grabbed Father's hand.
His father, Sheriff Brown, had killed
the Indian, who with one arm held Annie
by a shaft of hair, the other wielding
hatchet.

Sitting proud at the end of the table
was my mother's mother, Annie.

## Shadow

Below
the bluff,
barren
gray
trees:
simple,
precise.

Long,
lean
shadows,
the foliage
of life
discarded.

I remember
my grandmother,
erect,
eighty-five,
stripped
of life's
ornaments;
even her finger
lay bare,

her gold
wedding band
plucked
from her hand,
sold.

Bold high
cheekbones,
piercing
blue eyes.
Raw-boned
fingers
never at rest.

Long,
lean shadow

peaceful
at last.

## Sundays Below the Rocky Point

loom ash gray
all day.
Sundials forever
jammed
at dusk.
Granite churches,
spirited
solely
by mute
benches. Decorated
with bells,
bright gold,
never rung.
Silence broken
by hymns,
loud but unsung.
The Bishop
appears, God's
judge here on Earth.
His elegant wife,
in diamonds and mink.
Children age nine
standing, confessing.
Palpable guilt,
beware sins of omission.

## A Woman's Explanation to her Dead Father on Why She Marches Against the Bomb

Do you remember
when I was 10?
We raced across
parched salt flats
in your brand new convertible.

It was midnight,
bleak and black,
except for a canopy
of pulsing stars.
Cold air
like a knife's shining edge.
Only a shooting star could
match our speed
or lack of destination.

You were young and handsome.
We played hot jazz on the radio
and talked of UFOs,
interrupted only
by howling coyotes.

We were a time capsule
racing against light.
The black desert, a blanket,
hiding a picture:

Mother face down
on the floor,
You above her holding
a broken      bourbon      bottle.

## In the Crook of His Neck

Fine hairs on his shoulders gleam
like epaulets, reminding me of silk
mulberry threads Penelope used
for tapestries spun waiting
for her hero to come home.
We, women, always long for men
to step out of a myth or a Marlboro ad.

It begins all over again as he
caresses my back. I inhale the scent,
begin to relax. Once more I become
a defenseless girl wanting only
to close my eyes, bury my head
in the crook of his neck.

How old was I the first time,
possibly three? It happened
when Daddy came home. "Please
hold me, protect me, werewolves
are out, their eyes burning hot.
If you don't I know I will die."
I closed my eyes, buried
my head in the crook of his neck.

When I was sixteen, ripe but pure,
down by the arbor on a hot summer night,
my first beau's lips brushed mine. "My hero,
your Juliet's here." Pink tulle bound
my heart. I closed my eyes, buried
my head in the crook of his neck.

I am a grown woman, mother of men.
Experience fades; memory stills.
If only for a moment, I am saved.
My hero is here for maybe an hour,
willing to do battle, kill all my foes.
Illusions, myths, whatever is true.
I close my eyes, bury my head
in the crook of his neck.

## For Mother

### 1

Mother, at forty
you gave up
your last race,
let them bind rocks
to your feet.
Slowly, you sank deeper
into the glacier lake
of your body.
Because you raced,
breaking Olympic records,
no one believed
you could drown.

### 2

Medicine men believed
only your womb died.
True killers never punished.
Knowing youth
can never be reborn,
you made space
for your husband

to take a younger wife.
In the darkening
of your days,
your sliver moon
disappeared.
In stark rooms,
your brain numb,
doctors unhooked
your life.

3

Yesterday, in my house
I heard chimes bell forty...
pianissimo,
then fortissimo.
I am alone...
No one waits for my end.
Blood-red rosebuds,
snow-white dogwood
spring forth in
my garden.

## Anatomy of an Arranged Marriage

That night Mother hurled
an antique vase at my face.
It grazed the left cheek, shattered
the gilt mirror above the Adam mantle.

Two days later, she rang the papers,
threatened friends if they didn't disclose
my lair. Father demanded that police
issue warrants to drag me home
to glide down the aisle with this stranger.

As the sun mounted, abducting the fourth
night's safety, I stole into another cheap
motel. Worn down, I dreamed of John
the Baptist, saw King Herod hack off
his head. That night I stumbled home.

My father, without asking, gave his bond
to place my hand in his friend's wet palm.
The fifth time I saw him, my fiancé
slouched in grandfather's threadbare chair,
ran his fingers through thinning gray hair,
chortled at Father's shaded stories. Both
men swigged, got plastered. Mother caressed

my silk moiré dress, penciled in another
prominent guest. "The cake's been frosted
with your new name. We can't disappoint all
these people. Can we dear?"

Two weeks later friends, refused admission,
sent obelisk candlesticks to torch my path
to the altar. After the sealing, church ladies,
laden with massive trays, served a feast
in festive colors of mock-pink, blood-red.

That night I dreamed
of my long dark hair flowing
beneath the delicate lace veil.
My severed head crowned
a large silver platter.

## The Burning Tree

In the midst of a moonscape

by the Great Salt Lake

a burning

tree thrives.

During spring,

the tree

nourishes flame.

During summer,

it buries

deep pain.

During fall,

green hope

disappears.

The tree

of Sinai bursts

gold and red.

Crimson arrows

pointed skyward

giving back

to a world

its inhaled

sorrows

and tears.

## Pounding Dust

*"The dead living in their memories
are, I am persuaded, the source of
all that we call instinct."*

W. B. Yeats

1

In the summer when I run
the path between the canal
and the Potomac, my feet
pound dust: two sturdy hits
in accurate precision,
automatic metronomes, racing
to eclipse dusk. The glistening
runners I follow sprint beyond
memory. Rounding the two-
mile mark, inhaling wild
honeysuckle, minds white
out. Rhythmic peace leavens
longings for endless
hereditary thirsts:

Forefathers, marked
by cleft chins, their luck

with women. Rebels all: founders
of cities, avenging angels,
lovers of life, gallop through
my blood, storm my peace.
Their women: stoic, grieving
handmaidens, breathing
through children. Passwords
to daughters: savor every fruit
on every tree in the garden,
spark the fires, unbind my tongue.

2

The roar of the express train
from Lake Windemere to London hums.
Hypnotic rocking of the cars
lures ancient dreams. Recent
sights — the ancestral church,
the old stone home, family
gravestones, gentle generosities
of the land of my lineage — lull me.
In the distance I hear a song;
melodies burst fully formed
out of history. I am enveloped

by familiar strains never
heard before, begin to write
them down.

3

It is winter now.
Biting winds are silent
on the canal, reveal
tranquil waters beneath
a razor-thin layer
of ice. Guard-like trees
are winter-bared exposing
branches to light.
As I approach the locks,
water begins flowing.
Sunfish weave circuitous paths
from descending locks,
fall through small waterfalls
into the lowest pool.
Silt-bronzed maple leaves
dropped last autumn
remain intact below water,
lucid holograms
reflecting life.

# II.  SHATTERED HOUSES

*"Joe was beginning to know good from evil. And whoever does that is committed to live a human existence on this earth."*

Bruno Bettelheim

## Rituals

### 1

Sitting in a sidewalk
cafe on a steamy
Washington night,
I count out
nickels, dimes,
dollars into a
flower vendor's palm.
How tight
she fists the money.
How gaunt and
wary her body is.
Humped over,
dressed in black,
she takes each
rose:
pink, yellow, red,
layers them
over and over.

The waiter tells me
she's the only
family member

to survive
Nazi camps.
I see her
many years ago
in Auschwitz
carefully placing
roses over a mass grave:
pink, yellow, red.

2

For the last five days,
a cardinal has hurled
himself over and over
at my window.
Each day at dawn
I awake to a thud
as his body hits glass
like a ball
or a shot from a toy gun.

Is it like Narcissus
attempting to merge
with his mirror image?

Has spring fever
convinced him
the reflection
is a mate?
Is he his own enemy
protecting
the territory
from himself?

But a bird can fly away.

3

Faint and pale,
in a short white hospital
gown, her trembling hand
brushes kohl on her lids.
Fingers follow
the same curve
as a shaman sculpting
a mouth on a totem mask
or gods carving
a waning moon out
of a blackening sky.

Nurses think
how vain,
and wonder why
she would brush
Egyptian paint
on a naked face,
for her shadowed body
was slated to
meet no-one
but death.

## Brown Wrens

Beware of brown wrens.
Like blue jays,
they plunder nests,
suck yolk
from eggs,
while wearing
shetland sweaters,
round pearl pins.

So self-effacing,
they don't
even chirp
to give
secrets away.
They
attack
the closest nests.

One can peck
at the shell
of your life
until it shatters.

## Gauguin

I see you waiting
languorously
outside your pleasure
palace, leaning
on a cane clutched
with both hands,
scanning nubile
girls, their minds
vacuous
as a canvas
before you stroke
your brush.

You approve
each scarf-length
of hair as a piece
of goods.
Each breast,
will it fill
your hand
like a small melon
on the verge
of ripeness?

Each child
appraised
as an objet d'art
as indeed
she will become,
given your touch.

## Prodigal Fields

I. In the Heartland

For two centuries now,
Amish have nourished this land,
built fences high and well defined.
Ribbons of wheat bend melodically
in winds to fruitful rhythms.
Wearing black suits and hats,
men with beards falling down
to their chests
scythe harvests of grain.
Muslin-capped women
in long black aprons
clip along in carriages
behind cantering mares,
delivering freshly baked pies
to new mothers nursing babes.

In town,
tourists snap pictures,
snicker behind their hands
at an Amish mother and son
who turn alarmed faces
away from the camera,

stride around the corner
holding hands.

II. In the Piedmont

Since Lord Culpeper
granted land
to the Slaughter family
three hundred years ago,
only kin have plowed
this rich red earth.
Overnight, wild mushrooms
shoot up two feet high.
Blue grass grows dense,
dark as a rain forest.
Last year, drifting
over low fences
seeds germinated new ideas:
divorce took root
in fecund fields,
while on family lands
townhouses flowered.

Twelve-year-old Richard
seizes his mother's hand,
for they must hurry to the stream.
When they reach lower fields,
he spreads his arms:
"Look, Ma, you can see the farm
the way it was before you sold it.
Someday I'm going to buy it back
and if I can't...

I'll burn those houses down."

# A Peaceable Kingdom

*Rutherford, California, the heart of the wine country*

Sunset

Silence on the pond.

All the birds have disappeared.

A mangled goose,

its white feathers spangled with blood,

splayed out like a funeral wreath.

A mudhen, head severed,

all eggs gobbled from her nest.

The fox digs up their buried bodies

again and again.

The sun's blinding reflections

on the water appear

as iridescent sequins

on a slit satin dress

that a prostitute in the Tenderloin

wears to seduce.

## The Victims

*For Mary*

Each day, the mother braided
her daughter's golden hair:
plaiting the fragments of her
own hollow life through roots
into the child's fragile head.

When the mother's life withered,
too soon, — she was only forty-
one — her father, free, danced
down the aisle with the first ring moon.

After the groom lifted the bridal
veil, fondled his blossoming bride,
the daughter quaked, wailed into
the valley. She gulped the pills, sped
the car to a hill above the town, then
penned the note, "I'll soon be with my
mother; she'll never be alone again.
Signed, your loving daughter."

On the crest she breathed her last.
The warmth of death closed in slowly:
it felt just like her     mother.

## Mirage

He leaves
in the brassy light of dawn.
Into his blue tee-shirt
her shaky hand tucks a twenty.
Then her son is swallowed
through sunken doors.
His plane roars
past weightlessness,
like Icarus
soars toward the sun.
Pale knuckles
shift back into traffic.
Last year,
this unspoiled sixteen-year-old
didn't come home.
He reined his life
to California dreams,
spurred toward fast horses.
Like the stallions he rides,
his life thunders
toward barren fields.

On the mother's way home
from the airport,
stagnant light
of a hot June day descends.
Steam from the parkway envelops
her. A four-year-old blond head
lies in her lap. The child
still breathes deeply.

## A Day in Nantucket

The sand kept tripping the wheel.
You rode; I walked, pushing
the bicycle beside me. Do you
remember when we began the ride,
I fell off, skinned my knee?

On a wedgewood-blue afternoon,
we reached Dionis Beach.
At the far edge of the strand,
two isolated figures bent,
both clamming. A bar had risen
between the shore and sea.

You took my hand as our feet
sank into the boggy shore.
We walked, listened to seagulls
scold as they gorged on shellfish.

You told me of the time you thought
you had come upon ambergris,
how you buried what you believed
was treasure. After several days savoring
the find, you verified the secretion,
only to return and find it had washed away.

At the end of the beach, you told
me of pains in your chest the last
three days. In my mind, that sand bar
shifted mutely into place between
us. Black clouds began to form.

## Mother's Gift

Every day, her mother patiently

brushed Lisa's hair, long brown ringlets

falling half-way down her back.

How lovely she was.

Her mother mourned when she turned

twelve, became ungainly.

She dragged the child

to an ophthalmologist, orthopedist

and orthodontist. A surgeon even

offered to operate, straighten her aligned

spine. From then on Lisa wore:

glasses, lifts, braces.

Her mother stopped loving

her, asked "Is there anything

about you that's right?"


The dermatologist left the most lasting imprint;

he bombarded her average adolescent skin

with x-rays.


Twenty years later cancer cells appeared.

## Waiting for the X-Ray

Focus in

Focus out

Shutters blink

inside out.

Shadows stand at bay

then a light ray

flickers out.


Now the ghosts appear,

demons congregate.

Life turns inside out.

Look!  It slips away.

Focus in

Focus out

58

## Searching

Shale rocks
in the shape of a fist
appeared, then a sign selling fake
Apache artifacts flashed on the horizon.
Directly across was the Dry Creek Motel,
its tin roof blinding in the sun.
The phone whined.
Deserted streets; everyone hid
from scorching heat. Only vultures circled
in high sun as I dragged
myself to Pedro's Café to call you.

Three Doberman puppies snapped
while I carefully picked
my way up your gravel path,
trying to avoid rattlesnakes,
barbed wire. I pushed open the grating
door. Heavy curtains blackened
the room. Empty tequila bottles
appeared like kachina dolls
placed to cast a spell.
A grade B movie's shots
erupted from the television.
Puppies scavenged crumbs behind

chairs, squatted in dark corners.
Flies buzzed. The house reeked
of rotting food, cigarette stubs
left for weeks.

Your once chiseled
features were bloated. You limped
when you brought me iced tea, apologized
for not picking me up because your car
had been impounded. We couldn't unravel
the knots of the past, and as the hours ran,
I searched for the man I had once loved;
then, our son walked into the room.

## For Les

Father of my sons,

you are dying,

stretched out

on a starched sheet.

You lie      impotent,

lashed down by

life support systems.


Many years ago

a young girl

bound by religious duty

opened      her      legs

on a silken sheet,

waiting to conceive.

I,  at the beginning of life

and you at the end,

both pinioned

like dried butterflies.


How I wish I could help you fly.

## The County Fair

At sixteen,

her mother applauded

from the wings

as she was herded

onto the stage

to the beat

of a popular tune,

turning with grace

so judges would approve

breasts, buttocks, and face.

(They didn't look at teeth,

notice her quaking grimace.)

"Mighty pretty smile,

young lady. Want to

have dinner after the

show?" one judge asked,

then tried to pinch her hard.

The stallion waits in the barn.

## Wings

Last year,
I made peace
with my body.
Lying alone,
enveloped in space,
I began to unfold
from the fetal position.

I found I could
unbend each limb.
My arms spun out
to welcome worlds.
My legs craned straight,
pirouetting milky skies.

From each arm,
a wing blossomed.
At midnight, I would
soar serenely over
uncharted valleys,
mythical hills.
My vision knew no boundaries.

And then you came.
The tips of your fingers
drifted over my body.
Your arms encircled me.
Your kisses sealed my eyes.
My wings withered
and fell away.

Now, you are gone.
Again, I am rooted
in my cloistered body.
I pull up my legs,
wrap my arms
around my ribs
pretending my
own touch
is yours.

## Christina's Passion

*Based on Andrew Wyeth's painting,*
*"Christina's World"*

The sun
is too warm.
It is winter
here but
for an hour
or so a day
torrid
island pinks
linger.

Emblazoned
in this glow,
grass encased
in ice salivates.

Warm, white snow
softly seducing
her to come below.

She, forever
frozen
in heat
can't move.

The violet shadow
melts
becoming night.
Too late,
too late,
the sun has fled.

Nothing but crusted
ice now lies
below the snow.

# Lament

*for Carlotta Romney*
*(1925-1960)*

She kissed the boy's damp cheek,
smoothed his blond hair,
trod the steps past the barn
to the car.

In the old stone house,
behind leaded prisms
her husband stared.
She was stunned like a deer
blinded by light.
Her sweating hand fumbled for keys,
found the ignition,
gunned the car
toward the airport.

In an office overlooking
the bay,
her attorney said
"You can't go home.
You'll be killed.
Don't you understand

he's told his lawyer
you stole his gun?
He's planting an alibi."
Her body disappeared
into the black leather seat.

In a North Beach café,
spilled coffee burns her hand.
Startled, she remembers her son,
imagines him down at the barn.

Damn the devil.
The child is alone.
She must go back.

A weary blond boy
brushes his horse
one more time and hums,
"My Mother's coming home."

# On the First Day of Spring

1

A silent wind blows;

green wheat breaks earth.

The enigmatic source

of this fertility lures me.

When I attempt to cross your land,

barbed wire hooks my leg.

The jagged cut bleeds freely.

2

When I hold you,

I look into your eyes;

they are wild.

What are you afraid of,

my love—

of being snared

back into life?

## September in Nonquitt

Now the beach is still,
cleansed of people.
Only terns, ospreys, seagulls,
curve the edge of the shore.
Starkly etched against the sky,
rise the surrealistic rocks
that Heade touched with force.

Everyone sitting at this Chippendale
table sipping oyster stew has loved
in this grey-clapboard house.
Looking out the French doors, across
the terrace, past the ample lawn
through the elmed allee, beyond
those gray-brown sentinel rocks,
I can see their ancestors, sailing forth
in full-masted schooners from New
Bedford, Boston. Since 1872, their boats
have anchored in this cobalt bay, summer
shadowing summer. By candlelight,
darkening apparitions mirror my friends'
beaming faces on acid yellow walls: the same
aquiline noses, Dresden blue eyes.

A golden glow, an autumn chill on the ebbing
marsh, egrets feeding on sea life. Rosehips,
golden rod, primroses cloister
the road fashioned through the marsh coupling
South and North Nonquitt. A narrow canal
created to feed water in from the sea
is tapering down; I hear sighing tides.
The marsh is dying.
Only the rocks will attest.

# III. CIRCLING HOME

*"The moment freezes, compact whiteness that blinds and does not answer and dissolves, iceberg pushed by circular currents. It must return."*

Antonio Paz

## To My Eighteen-Year-Old Son

A squall has risen
the last day
in my rented house
at the beach.
It bends several sheltering
pines to reveal
a small statue
of a boy about ten
secreted away behind
the English garden.

I remember when
you were that age;
I wanted to bonsai you.
The best I could do
was to take photographs.

I run my fingers over
the cold brow
of the statue,
kiss its rough cheek,
look into those unseeing
eyes and, for a moment,
find you again.

## Taking Leave of the Farm

Morning blanches white.

The sun shimmers

above the elusive green

hills I love.

Thick wet fog entombs

my flesh.

The heat of dying summer

swathes my bones.

Am I Persephone

sucked into inner earth,

cradled but chained?

I must leave Eden

but this eternal visceral

trap won't spring my body free.

Lush, southern land clings

to me. I am seared and trapped

by Paradise,

lost     again,

     this     time     deliberately.

## One Cold Icy Day

in the country

when all is silver,

gray, hidden,

overnight

a green blaze

of winter wheat

flames into sight,

flares to touch the sun,

a surrealistic

ribbon of life

wrapping the furrows

with banners,

a streak of chutzpah,

like a brash green man

too soon reaching

to touch you,

wanting to bring

you spring.

Over-anxious,

over-reaching.

At first you're shocked,

then pleased.


You thaw.

## Across a Roman Piazza

The stranger's gaze
burns across the piazza
refracting the sun's rays
on a dry willow.

I feel his touch.
He smooths his fine hair;
silk flows through my fingers.
I smell the fragrance of skin
after a summer storm.

I nod at my friend
who sits across the table
and try to listen,
but his stare
commands my presence.

He leans forward
as if to get a better view,
although he is forty feet away
I know his eyes
are Mediterranean blue.

We have made love
in a shadow
of the Via Veneto
and danced naked
on the road to Amalfi
nine centuries ago.

## The Embrace

How strange to be embraced

from within: an enveloping

velvet, the sweetness of honey,

a schism of time,

a communing with nature,

a soft Rubens' flush.

Let youth have its drama,

my lover, my sweet.

I live for our moments,

gentle, complete.

## Lifelines

A woman arches her brow,

gazes into a mirror,

feels a warm blush

flood her cheek,

a harbinger of frost,

which will soon shrivel

her breasts.

After drying her face,

she brings her hands slowly

to her eyes.

The lifelines curving

her palms have fulfilled their lot:

planted vegetables, pulled weeds,

folded clothes, washed beans,

caressed children's fevered heads.

Brown spots mark her wise.

The swelling rivers of blue

boldly cry *endure.*

## The Arc

A pale blue wire
binds sky to sea.

The arc of his
smile hooks
my body

anchoring me
to earth.

## Connections

On the Mediterranean shore

you watch the scarlet legs

of the Chianti climb

almost to the rim

then fall back

into the bottom

of the glass.

The other hand balances a telephone.

Your words, "I need you"

ricochet off a satellite

across night skies to San Francisco.

2

An unfettered mare is startled

when heat lightning blazes

across Utah skies.

Claps of thunder reverberate

through Glenn Canyon.

The horse prods red dust to find footing,

bolts for the cleft of the gorge,

runs aimlessly

until immersing herself

in the Snake River;

she herds rapids as water drags

stones toward Hoover Dam.

The malachite fingers

of lake splay out, gripping

the Paleozoic rust body of the desert.

As the mare quenches her thirst,

the river and torrents of storms

gather deep in the crater's core

later surge over the dam,

plummet through arid reaches

of New Mexico, Arizona, then

to burgeon in California,

nurture deep root stock, fan out vines,

swell garnet grapes.

3

I drain the last drop

of Cabernet from the glass,

put down the telephone and smile.

# Climbing Mount St. Helena in August

We scale Mount St. Helena
in midday; fatigue of unremitting
heat takes hold. A madrone
offers partial shade
as we rest briefly, talk
of whom you've loved
and why. We begin again;
cliffs spiraling up.
Staccato of pulses
quicken. I struggle
for breath. Our eyes stalk
the mountain to see the vaulting
summit. I question
myself, when did I love,
how did it fall away?

We crest, aim
our cameras to capture
this view we've earned.
Below us, copper hills cradle
verdant valleys. Braids
of red and green grapestock
appear as waves on the sea
lulling instincts to sleep.
In the distance, gliders float
silently above Calistoga.
Passengers hang in baskets, balloons:
suspended dolls awaiting life.

## Beauty and Birth

*for Sibyl and Sandra*

Brightly,
our enchanted
vision burns.
Wild floral
images reflect
women.
In the mist,
gardenias, irises
glow. At times,
forgotten, still
orchids appear.
Hyacinths breathe
in the snow.
Saguaro flowers
in sand.
Cereus spring
to life deep
in the night.
Passion shades
enduring
wellsprings.

The feminine
nucleus
forms the earth,
the mouth
of being,
the mystique
of quickening.

## And then Daybreak

*"...And then rain fell upon the earth for forty days and forty nights...At the end of forty days, Noah opened the window of the ark and sent forth a dove but the dove found no place to set her foot..." Genesis, 7-8*

After circling storms
night after night,
all soft feathers stripped
from beating wings,
the dove finds no
refuge. She spins, lost
over expanses of rising
waters, surging tides,
plummets into shrieking
winds, her cries muted.

Desperately aching,
I am chilled
by darkening,
sob throughout
the night,
pleading for rest.

Moments before dawn,
the dove sights land.
I hear a fluttering
of wings on the roof.

And then daybreak, my hand  finds  yours.

## Through My Secret Garden

*"Desire is full of endless distances"*

*Robert Hass*

1

The early spring sun
reverberates on light blue walls.
An old ceiling fan whirs,
arousing memories as I slip naked
between crisp sheets. I remember
thirteen-year-old bodies lying
on a delft blue quilt under
a thicket of leaves: my friend
leans on one arm, whispers
what older boys and girls do
in the back seats of cars.
He presses his leg against
mine, smoothes back the fine
hair on my arm.

## 2

Lying in my four-poster bed
on a balmy June evening, I kick
off the heavy down comforter.
Honeyed fragrance of a tender
breeze kisses my cheek.
Sounds of silky laughter
float up from a sidewalk
café, caress my thigh.
Moonlight filtered through louvers
throws a mosaic of his body
on the azure wall. The window
at the head of my bed is a matchmaker
ushering in my love.

3

For years beyond counting
behind luminous screens
of Pompeian blue,
my desire
like a kite serpentining
over white trees
floated on the sea's breath;
then in September, the bay
air crisped; the mandarin
moon vanished. Desire
lifted and arced
in the hawk wind
as a spirited woman
would take her lover
until it crashed, spun
recklessly, imprisoned
in the arms of trees.

4

In late November, I open
my door and step
onto a road
garlanded with gold
coins. Georgetown
is strewn with gingko
leaves, fallen
from trees as
in the Bible,
as old as Joseph's
rainbow robe.
I will cover myself
with this golden
treasure as Eve
wore her leaves
in the Garden;
I will loosen
my auburn hair
and let it fall
past my waist, but
I will not speak
to snakes.

## Games

*Upon reaching a significant birthday*

I embrace my age

as a gambler her game.

Each new hand

exacts a score:

an illusion, a lover,

one day: my life.

Reshuffle the decades:

it's my turn to deal.

I swallow my losses,

wager my dreams,

see my children lose

their highest bids,

finesse beauty

to live another day,

count my trumps

in the year of hearts,

bluff my way

toward tomorrow.

## Smiles

Bones mesh;

length and weight

fit into one.

In the dark of night,

the curve of spines

are      like      one

generous      smile

curved around another.

# Orestean Rite

*"...the myriad tribes of the dead came thronging up with a wondrous cry, and pale fear seized me, lest august Persephone might send forth upon me from out of the house of Hades, the head of the Gorgon, that awful monster." The Odyssey XI*

Bruised — chosen — damned
Sucked into depths
by a lover's leaving.
Entrapped in Medusa's undertows
of fatigue.
Drowned in oblivion
striving to stay alive.
All sisters, brothers, unto the deep,
tempted      to      sink.

Pull — Pull — Pull
Swim through pain;
squint red eyes.
Clutch slick seaweed
with wrinkled hands.
Tread water
and watch
and wait.

Clasp at last
an even tide of peace
where cool water laps.
Victory kisses ever sweeter.
Float beyond the reef
where white whales sing,
dolphins dive through
Poseidon's wreath:

Healed

Chosen

Blessed

## Circling Home

As the plane ascends western skies,
out of the window, a bald eagle
loops the horizon. Below, a Pawnee
chief with his wizened forefinger
traces the Indian sign for home,
a nest, in sand.

In our American cycle of seasons,
we endlessly quest for our own place
as a child seeks its mother's
breast. Like gypsies, we tent
for a day, grow restless, strike
the canvas, move on to an unknown
city, smile at a stranger we have
yet to befriend, embrace
an idea we do not comprehend.

The plane tracks the span of
America, scans the continental
divide. I peer down; identify
bold deserts, fruitful prairies,
the meandering Mississippi, Virginia,
places I have lived; remember people
I care for. Tonight, the plane
homes in on Washington.

# NOTES

Inherit the Promise: In Salt Lake City, Utah, there is a monument to the seagull. The bird is credited with saving the city from a locust plague in 1848.

Sundays Below the Rocky Point: In the Mormon Church, the Church of Latter Day Saints, the ministry is made up of male laymen.

September in Nonquitt: Martin Heade, an American 19th century Luminist painter, painted numerous seascapes emphasizing rock formations along the beach.

# BIOGRAPHIES

Cheryl Romney-Brown was born in Salt Lake City, Utah, of a Mormon Pioneer heritage. She went back to college after having her family and received a bachelor of arts degree from Hutchins College and her master's degree in liberal arts from Georgetown University in 1986. At Georgetown, she began writing poetry, and was the first person allowed to submit a manuscript of poetry in lieu of a dissertation. Shortly thereafter, the manuscript was displayed, as the example of a contemporary poet who had been influenced by William Wordsworth, in the "William Wordsworth and the Age of Romanticism" exhibit. She is currently working on a forthcoming novel, "The Second Son of the Seventh Wife," for which she received a fellowship from the Virginia Center for the Creative Arts. She has also published poems in: *Whetstone, Visions, Pulpsmith, Late Knocking, Ploughshares,* and the *1985 American Poetry Anthology.*

Pamela Soldwedel is a native New Yorker, who studied sculpture as an undergraduate at Bennington College, Vermont. Thereafter she pursued a varied career in New York City and New Mexico. Only after moving to Washington, D.C., in the mid-1970s did Soldwedel resume her sculpture, studying at the Corcoran School of Art with Berthold Schmutzhart. At the Corcoran in 1980 she won the Martha von Hirsh Award and the Mary Lay Thom Sculpture Award for Most Outstanding Work. She has exhibited her sculpture in numerous shows and is included in corporate and private collections throughout North America, many of them through special commission.

# Scripta humanistica

*Directed by*
BRUNO M. DAMIANI
*The Catholic University of America*
COMPREHENSIVE LIST OF PUBLICATIONS *

| | | |
|---|---|---|
| 1. | Everett W. Hesse, *The "Comedia" and Points of View.* | $24.50 |
| 2. | Marta Ana Diz, *Patronio y Lucanor: la lectura inteligente "en el tiempo que es turbio."* Prólogo de John Esten Keller. | $26.00 |
| 3. | James F. Jones, Jr., *The Story of a Fair Greek of Yesteryear.* A Translation from the French of Antoine-François Prévost's *L'Histoire d'une Grecque moderne.* With Introduction and Selected Bibliography. | $30.00 |
| 4. | Colette H. Winn, *Jean de Sponde: Les sonnets de la mort ou La Poétique de l'accoutumance.* Préface par Frédéric Deloffre. | out of print |
| 5. | Jack Weiner, *"En busca de la justicia social: estudio sobre el teatro español del Siglo de Oro."* | $24.50 |
| 6. | Paul A. Gaeng, *Collapse and Reorganization of the Latin Nominal Flection as Reflected in Epigraphic Sources.* Written with the assistance of Jeffrey T. Chamberlin. | $24.00 |
| 7. | Edna Aizenberg, *The Aleph Weaver: Biblical, Kabbalistic, and Judaic Elements in Borges.* | $25.00 |
| 8. | Michael G. Paulson and Tamara Alvarez-Detrell, *Cervantes, Hardy, and "La fuerza de la sangre."* | $25.50 |
| 9. | Rouben Charles Cholakian, *Deflection/Reflection in the Lyric Poetry of Charles d'Orléans: A Psychosemiotic Reading.* | $25.00 |
| 10. | Kent P. Ljungquist, *The Grand and the Fair: Poe's Landscape Aesthetics and Pictorial Techniques.* | out of print |
| 11. | D.W. McPheeters, *Estudios humanísticos sobre la "Celestina."* | $20.00 |
| 12. | Vittorio Felaco, *The Poetry and Selected Prose of Camillo Sbarbaro.* Edited and Translated by Vittorio Felaco. With a Preface by Franco Fido. | $25.00 |
| 13. | María del C. Candau de Cevallos, *Historia de la lengua española.* | $33.00 |
| 14. | *Renaissance and Golden Age Studies in Honor of D.W. McPheeters.* Ed. Bruno M. Damiani. | out of print |
| 15. | Bernardo Antonio González, *Parábolas de identidad: Realidad interior y estrategia narrativa en tres novelistas de postguerra.* | $28.00 |
| 16. | Carmelo Gariano, *La Edad Media (Aproximación Alfonsina).* | $30.00 |
| 17. | Gabriella Ibieta, *Tradition and Renewal in "La gloria de don Ramiro".* | $27.50 |
| 18. | *Estudios literarios en honor de Gustavo Correa.* Eds. Charles Faulhaber, Richard Kinkade, T.A. Perry. Preface by Manuel Durán. | $25.00 |
| 19. | George Yost, *Pieracci and Shelly: An Italian Ur-Cenci.* | $27.50 |
| 20. | Zelda Irene Brooks, *The Poetry of Gabriel Celaya.* | $26.00 |

## BOOK ORDERS

* Clothbound. *All book orders*, except library orders, must be prepaid and addressed to **Scripta Humanistica**, 1383 Kersey Lane, Potomac, Maryland 20854. *Manuscripts* to be considered for publication should be sent to the same address.